VIA FOLIOS 109

Reverse Graffiti

Also by Joey Nicoletti

Borrowed Dust (2011)
Earthquake Weather (2012)
Cannoli Gangster (2012)
Shadow Traffic (2014)

Reverse Graffiti

Poems

Joey Nicoletti

BORDIGHERA PRESS

Library of Congress Control Number: 2015937927

COVER PHOTO: Mary Beth Sullivan

Printed in the United States.

Published by
BORDIGHERA PRESS
John D. Calandra Italian American Institute
25 West 43rd Street, 17th Floor
New York, NY 10036

VIA FOLIOS 109
ISBN 978-1-59954-087-0

ACKNOWLEDGEMENTS

Grateful acknowledgement is made to the editors of the following journals, in which some of these works first appeared, sometimes in different forms:

The Adroit Journal: The Firmament
Aethlon: To Rafael Soriano
Blue Lake Review: Death Star Summer, The Spot
Green Hills Literary Lantern: Earthquake Weather
Heron Tree: Onion Pie
H.O.D.: Blues for Darth Vader, Fly Song, Old World Soufflé, Sleeping with the Dog, Under the Milky Way, Winter Lager
In Bantam: The Neptune Factor
Italian Americana: To Joe Pepitone
Italian Americana Online: Diane di Prima Day
Jet Fuel Review: The Family Hitman
Meadowland Review: Brand New Cadillac
Oklahoma Review: The Death of Captain Marvel, The Death of Boba Fett
The Potomac: K-Ville Renovated Love, Red Eye Blues
Southwestern American Literature: At the Trinity Site, Balloons Over the Sandias, Falsetto Sky
Sou'wester: Shadow Traffic
Stymie Magazine: Avenue of the Americas
Sunken Lines: It's Tricky, What Ringo Starr Taught Me
Two Bridges Review: Classic TV
Valparaiso Poetry Review: Reverse Graffiti, Risotto Elegy
Voices in Italian Americana: Che Gelida Manina
Waccamaw: Condemned Hospital Elegy, The Flashlight Fish
Blue Train appeared in the anthology *Token Entry: New York Subway Poems,* Smalls Press, 2012.

Lee Smith appeared in the anthology *City of the Big Shoulders: An Anthology of Chicago Poetry,* University of Iowa Press, 2012.

Shadow Traffic appeared in the anthology *Small Batch: An Anthology of Bourbon Poetry,* Winged City Press, 2013.

Trey Anastasio at Red Rocks Amphitheatre appeared in the anthology *Lipsmack! A Sampler Platter of Poets from NightBallet Press: Year Two, 2013.*

The Death of Captain Marvel and What John Romita, Sr. Taught Me appeared in the anthology *Drawn to Marvel: Poems from the Comic Books,* Minor Arcana Press, 2014.

The Flashlight Fish appeared in the anthology *Rabbit Ears: TV Poems,* Poets Wear Prada Press, 2015.

Transplant originally appeared on the blog site *200 New Mexico Poems: One Hundred Poems Celebrating the Past, One Hundred More Celebrating the Future,* in April 2012.

Brand New Cadillac appeared in the anthology *Clash by Night: Lo-Fi Poetry,* City Lit Books, 2015.

Some of the poems first appeared in the poetry chapbooks *Earthquake Weather* and *Shadow Traffic.* NightBallet Press published the former in 2012 and the latter in 2014.

I also want to thank all of the following friends, colleagues, and fellow poets who helped in the making of this book: my spouse, Beth Sullivan; Dianne Borsenik; Stacy Lynn Brown; Claudia Emerson; Stacia M. Fleegal; Fred Gardaphé; Amy Glynn; George Guida; Rachel Guido deVries; Kate Knapp Johnson; Gerry LaFemina; Thomas Lux; Maria Mazziotti Gillan; Alan Shapiro; Vijay Seshadri; Anthony Julian Tamburri; Kathleene West; Chloe Yelena Miller.

Grazie di cuore!

For Mary Elizabeth Sullivan.

And in memory of Claudia Emerson
(1957–2014)

TABLE OF CONTENTS

Reverse Graffiti

ONION PIE

The wind, the rattling wall, dinner
baking in the oven, the dead of winter
a string of salt diamonds
alight in a street of slush and moonlit ice,
and the cat retires
to his feathery bed.

I'm the child who's read
every issue of the Amazing Spider Man:
I spin webs of all shapes and sizes
in my sleep, on and off the page,
to capture the nebulous villains of memory and tradition
who would otherwise evade or defeat me.

I investigate my mother's stories
about her childhood in Orsogna, Italia.
The latest case: Lisa,
my mother's kid sister,
who went to school one day and didn't
return. Three army soldiers stormed
into her classroom.
Reeking of pipe smoke and wine,
they demanded everyone's jewelry,
including the teacher's
for the war effort. The class obeyed.

The soldiers sang
"Il Canto degli Italiani,"
then left, and set
the school ablaze.
The fire fighters saved some
of the children.
Lisa wasn't one of them.
I 've never seen a picture of her.

Thus, the character Almost Aunt Lisa has appeared
in my life like a phantom
in the mausoleum of my imagination.
My Mother, Nonno
Giovanni, and Nonna Ida were in America;
Astoria, New York, 11 months later.

My mother's recollections of the journey were limited
to adjectives and events:
long, cramped, vile;
a cousin and an uncle dead.
The cause:
Malaria. Maybe Scurvy.
Death had a clammy grip
on the forehead and the heart.

Since we've been partners,
my wife and I have tried
to find the answers together.
We have yet to fill in all of the blanks
of the blue-exam-books

of our respective cultural and familial histories.
Mastering recipes is the closest we've come
to a thoroughly successful search.

Tonight features a succulent trip
to the old country;
a buttery, spicy-sweet taste of Italia:
I pull the Onion Pie out of the oven,
my face kissed by steam.

THE DEATH OF CAPTAIN MARVEL

– after the Graphic Novel by Jim Starlin

When Captain Marvel died,
the stars became
splotches of detergent.
When Captain Marvel died
of cancer, my candy-cigarette days
smoldered in my father's ashtray.
When Captain Marvel died,
my Uncle's tour bus stalled on bridges
gripped in frost and soot.
I was a cracked fire hydrant,
calling out my big sister's name
in my watery dialect.
I was a pair of boots, an olive-green and yellow
pair of rubber boots who slipped
on a sidewalk being fitted
in a new see-through dress of ice.
I was a soccer ball
with a small hole, losing air slowly,
like my mother was
in her hospital room.
When Captain Marvel, the most
cosmic super hero of all died,
he was surrounded by family and friends,

like my mother was
in her final days. A few pages
before Captain Marvel died,
Spider-Man abruptly walked out
of the Captain's chambers, overcome
by shock and disbelief. I saw my face
beneath his mask: blood-shot
eyes dilated with the awful fear of death;
his head looking backwards, like mine
in Mount Sinai Hospital;
breathless, defenseless, no web to spin,
only sweaty palms:
one to place on my sister's shoulder,
the other to rub my eyes
after we said our goodbyes;
my sister and I walking down a hallway
of dim, sickly light.

SHADOW TRAFFIC

A bottle of white, a bottle of red.
Whenever I hear Billy Joel sing
this lyric, I am seven years old
again, wrapping myself around
my mother's swollen ankles,
trying to keep her
from beating my big sister
with a metal bat. Her rage fueled
by Riunite Lambrusco and long hours
at work to keep Con Ed solvent,
I can't stop her. My father is stuck
in traffic, listening in horror
as Reggie Jackson and Billy Martin
come to blows in Fenway Park.
A bottle of red, a bottle of white.
This lyric returns me to the night
before I left home for good;
before I lost my accent
like a fly ball in an afternoon sun.
My father and I watch the Yankees play
against the Blue Jays. Joe Carter blasts
a Scott Sanderson deuce into the net
above Monument Park. A breeze nudges
my mother's wedding portrait on the wall.
A Camel cigarette smolders in an ashtray.

The Yankees season is dead, my father says,
just like your mother, my wife. I hear him cough
for minutes on end for the first time.
I'm fine, he says. I wouldn't trade this night
for anything, unlike you, my son.
He sips his bourbon, then hands me a glass of water:
This is so your plane ticket doesn't burn
too big of a hole in your pocket, he says.
You were right, Father: I swapped shadows
of skylines and sound walls
for those of mountains and mesas.
My mother. Your wife.

CHE GELIDA MANINA

– after Puccini

The day my sister ran away,
My mother chopped onions.
The gas grill trembled in its suit of armor
When she stomped onto the patio.

My mother chopped onions.
Luciano Pavarotti crackled from the hi-fi
As mounds of my father's sweaters burned
Like dinner for lavender May sky.

Luciano Pavarotti crackled from the hi-fi,
Sedan doors slammed shut in driveways.
Our tulips guzzled sunlight and water
Like Mr. McClure's potted begonias next door.

Sedan doors slammed shut in driveways:
The gas grill trembled in its suit of armor
Like Mr. McClure's potted begonias next door
The day my sister ran away.

THE FLASHLIGHT FISH

or George, as I called him, stood out
like a Green Lantern decoder ring
on TV, with glands that glowed
 just below each eye. I watched him
enter a watery room
with a shy smile. He blinked
for his next meal
in the shadow of a Caribbean night.
What I liked best about George
was how comfortable he was in his own skin;
how willing he was to share himself with others,
unlike me, having rejected
John Kingman's invitation
to dinner at his house
because he kissed me on the mouth
underneath the monkey bars
earlier in the day. I saw George and a school
of his brothers and sisters
assist a ship through a coral reef passage,
twisting and turning a crew of hired hands to safety.
Then my thoughts washed up on the surface:
I imagined my father,
driving home from the bus depot
after another graveyard shift of picking
passengers up and dropping them off

throughout the city; his back and legs sore,
our house looming in the headlights
as he pulled into the driveway,
moonlight oozing into the nights of his hands.

CLASSIC TV

8:00 pm. My cat stares me down
from the apartment window as I get out
of the car. The milky light
pouring from the big dipper
does not appear
to have quenched his thirst:
it took its time to get here, as opposed to me,
a servant to routine; my stomach
snarling its demand for dinner
as I ran a red light, paying no mind
to the cop on the corner;
the station wagon pulling out of its driveway
before I took my final turn home.
I look into the sliding doors
of the living room below mine:
Mary Tyler Moore throws her hat
in the dusty air of the TV screen. I hear
wind chimes harmonize on porches.
A pothole overflows with moonlight
in the grass. I drop my keys.
Satellite dishes sag
in the muddy ground.

CONDEMNED MENTAL HOSPITAL ELEGY

The musk of iodine stings
the thick summer air.
I stare into a hallway
of smog. I see
bruised fingers dialing pay phones
to call their loved ones,
helpless as water faucets;
my Uncle Frank's face rising
from his meaty hands:
a bearded sun
over the cityscape of ash trays and Dixie cups
on his table in the visiting center
when my father and I pull up a chair.
The neon of the convenience store
sign across the street
flashes *MIGHTY SHOP*
into a puddle of oil. I put the key
in my sea-green hatchback's scratched ignition.
Factory smoke gathers
like street gangs in my rearview mirror.

THE NEPTUNE FACTOR

— after the film by Daniel Petrie

Dear Ben Gazzara,
your Southern accent fooled no one.
Starlight squirms like a headless eel
in the bottom of the Atlantic.

When a superimposed goldfish stares
in your submarine window, I cannot suspend
my disbelief, despite your cast-mates' college tries
to feign expressions of wonder and surprise in their eyes.

You can take an Italian boy out of the Bronx,
but the fire escapes of Arthur Avenue
cling to the building of your semi-trained tongue
like rust on ladders;

like soot on the screen of the decrepit drive-in
where I first saw you; your face now in a place
where only the man in the moon can come up for air,
smirking the weeds out of the theatre grounds.

TO JOE PEPITONE

My father's hair dryer turns its lonely eye to you.
Your home-run swing
and your Sicilian lineage
made his Egg Creams all the sweeter;

going to bed as if it was a bottom bunk
in Rikers Island, until he met my mother.
Then there was Vietnam.
You gave him something to cheer about

with your gold gloves; your pair of toupees,
one for sweet-talking the ladies
under the glare of disco balls,
and one for underneath your cap;

your *game-piece*; the one that came loose
when you took your cap off
for the national anthem. River Avenue
fire hydrants bite their corroded lips.

TRANSPLANT

The dialect of the Sandias shatters
in World Trade Center window glass
on CNN. Jet streams scar

the Rio Rancho sky,
with high tide inevitable
back east. My father drives

his bus in Bed-Stuy.
My worries jump out
the smoldering floor

of the first tower.
I call his cell phone again:
dial tones engulf my living room.

RED EYE BLUES

Airport Security. Gloved hands slide
toward my groin. I step aside
at a thick-necked officer's command.

My Converse kicks call out my name
in red suede concern.
I do what I can to comply,

but I make no apologies
for my olive-skin;
my peasant hands, gnarled and callused,

like those of my grandparents and uncles
when they raised the GW, the Whitestone,
the Verrazano, and the Triborough:

the bridges of their hopes, dreams,
loves and other assorted disasters.
The officer continues:

he pats my legs again,
glaring the denim off of my jeans;
the numbers off of my football jersey.

A grope here, a shove there,
a monotone sentence of thanks
for my cooperation.

And as I bite my tongue,
I spot a nub on his right hand,
where his index finger should be.

Maybe the officer's disposition is a matter
of being proactive;
of pushing away the pain

of what's been lost.
Perhaps his sadness takes cover
in gloves of pale-blue regulations

as a way of protecting himself
from the windblown grains
of memory's dunes;

a way of keeping safe
from the friendly fire of everyday life;
of moving on

from the thick skin of combat
forged halfway around the world.
So I nod, grab my carry-on,

then step into my kicks,
and I feel a quiet pouring, like cream
into a cup of coffee

behind the Starbuck's counter
up ahead of me,
like the day itself.

I look out a window:
tall, distant trees sway.
A plane waits on the runway.

K-VILLE RENOVATED LOVE

Like the workshop of a carpenter,
the wiry sky is full of buzz saws,
and our love is a wood panel, split
in half after the walls of our home were pried off
by the crowbars of water
after the levees broke.
Our bodies are full of cats and dogs:
none of them have a home,
only images: on TV, cyberspace, or papers
stapled into telephone poles
fractured like my brother's leg
after a bombing in downtown Baghdad.
Shaggy-haired volunteers descend
on the New Orleans streets.
Scratched hammers peek out of rusty toolboxes,
as if eyeing the packages of nails stacked on front stoops.
They are silvery,
a new kind of punctuation;
upside-down periods and exclamation points
for our the revised essay of our digs,
the structure of fresh air
we might breathe and speak again.

AT THE TRINITY SITE

I saw displays of charcoal drawings of mushroom clouds dang
from barbed-wire fences scaling the dusty air
and thought about the machinists and physicists
who spent their time here thinking of new ways
to trigger mechanisms, to weep in intricate grids.

A man behind me pointed at one of the drawings and said,
That'll look great under the moose head!
and swaggered into the rest of his life.
My thoughts toppled, like the tree trunks
half-buried in the sand beyond the fence.

Risotto Elegy

The day crushed me
like a grape in its green pain as I read
a few words about my Uncle Enzo
at his funeral mass. My voice cracked
as I tried to decipher my handwriting.
The windows rattled a stained-glass hymn
when an airplane flew above the church. I wondered
if its passengers were shuffling in their seats
as nervously as my relatives were in the pews.
Then we went to a bistro around the corner.
Our whistles wet with Chianti,
everyone told Uncle Enzo stories, even my Aunt
Zia, his widow, who usually said
yes as a long answer to a question.
No was her short one.
She talked about the time he tried
to build a campfire in their backyard
by rubbing my brother's Lincoln Logs together.
My mother's hapless sigh rose in steam
from her plate of risotto,
her attention divided
between Aunt Zia and the crash
of broken plates; an off-key choir
scattered in the kitchen
like Uncle Enzo's ashes in the East River,
telephone wires stitching the sky.

THE FAMILY HITMAN

—RE: Chuckie "The Typewriter" Nicoletti, 1916-1977

I am a pistol, filled
with water, squirting my brother in the eyes
when he falls asleep watching The Brady Bunch.
I am the red nylon, textured
Mo Cheeks jersey in the cheap seats
of Madison Square Garden.
I am the name and date written
in chicken scratch, on the card
of the overdue library book.
I am not the gold horn, dangling
from the 14 karat chains
of my uncles and cousins.
I am not one of the mechanics
who fired at JFK
from behind a picket fence in Dallas.
I am not alone, not the recipient
of three bullets to the back of my head while waiting
in a sedan, before it catches fire,
keys rattling against the lacquered dash.

DIANE DI PRIMA DAY

Diane, I couldn't agree more
with your choices for having days
of celebration for our people.

Among those choices:
Ani Di Franco Day.
Gregory Corso Day.

Lawrence Ferlinghetti Day.
Sacco and Vanzetti Day.
Sacco and Vanzetti Day.

Philip Lamantia Day.
Julie Bovasso Day.
Martin Scorsese Day.

I'd like to add a few more nominations,
if I may. Quentin Tarantino Day.
Nancy Pelosi Day.

I'd like to say
Antonin Scalia Day
or Samuel Alito Day, but I can't,

as I believe in a woman's right to choose,
and I believe
that you do, too.

In addition to Joe DiMaggio Day,
let us not forget
others in his clan, extended and blood alike:

Dom DiMaggio Day.
Vince DiMaggio Day.
Marilyn Monroe Day.

Though she and Joe split up,
who could truly wear
the red, white, and green

or red, white, and anything
or nothing
better than she?

While we're on the subject of famiglia:
Dino and Giada de Laurentis Day.
Mario Andretti and sons Day.

I gotta give mad props
to my other thespian peeps
who have made me see my own clan

more clearly, the world differently.
So, tanti saluti: here's to
Ray Liotta Day.

Lorraine Bracco Day.
Mira Sorvino Day.
Anne Bancroft Day.

Molto grazie times infinity.
Edie Falco Day.
Steve Buscemi Day.

Giovanni Ribsi Day.
John Cazale Day.
Abe Vigoda Day.

Sofia Coppola Day.
Heather Matarazzo Day.
Talia Shire Day — the film madre

of Sage Moonblood Stallone;
the film moglie of Sly;
Sylvester Stallone Day.

"Titanic" notwithstanding, his philanthropy abounding,
Leonardo DiCaprio Day.
John Turturro Day.

It doesn't seem hyperbolic to say
that many of my pubescent days
involved Madonna in some way.

Judging by the Twitterverse alone,
today could mos def be Lady Gaga Day.
OMG. Trey Anastasio Day.

I'll step to the plate
for Rocky Colavito Day.
Tony Conigliaro Day.

Same goes for Ron Santo Day.
Joe Torre Day.
Rocco Baldelli Day.

Since John Franco told me
to go fuck myself
when I asked him for an autograph

politely, at Shea Stadium, when I was 14,
I have since decreed that September 17th,
his birthday, is *Bafongool Day*.

I gotta give it up
for Lee Mazzilli Day.
Rico Petrocelli Day.

When I was a kid, Sunday was for dinner,
church, and the NFL: Mark Bavaro Day.
Brian Piccolo Day.

I live la dolce vita when I read
comics drawn by John Romita, Senior
Peter Parker never looked better.

Big John Buscema Day: grazie for the Vision.
Our Pal Sal Buscema: grazie for Spider-Woman.
Carmine Infantino Day: grazie for the Silver-Age Flash.

I live la dolce vita when I read your words
and ideas, so I would be remiss not to say
Diane di Prima day.

Helen Barolini Day.
Don DeLillo Day.
Camille Paglia Day.

Tom Perrotta Day.
Richard Russo Day.
Rachel Guido DeVries Day.

This is also a call for
Jon Fante Day.
Mario Puzo Day.

As I say, I couldn't agree more:
Sacco and Vanzetti Day.
Sacco and Vanzetti Day.

One more round;
one last toast of thanks
for inspiration and activism:

Diane di Prima Day.
Diane di Prima Day. All day.
All night. I choose.

TO RAFAEL SORIANO

Stare into your cap
before you put in on.
Glare at your catcher
if you don't get the save.
Glare at your catcher
if you do, then un-tuck your jersey
immediately.
I don't know if you have the same look
when you're eating a steak;
I don't know if you'll be back
next year. You're not Mo Rivera,
nor do you need to be.
Keep mixing the four-seamer
with the sharp slider.
Keep enjoying the end of a day's work,
like my wife, as she slams the door of her SUV
in the starlit parking lot.

SLEEPING WITH THE DOG

The moon has been buried in the yard.
The electric blanket of morning warms up
as he climbs into bed, then plops down

beside me. The chain saw of his snoring cuts
the trees of the graveyard shift's frustrations
down to size: every branch and stump

a leafless complaint; a bark-less demand.
I drift on a river of slumber and look up
from my gondola of exhaustion:

the sky is as pink as his tongue, ready
to lick me awake; to remove the sleepers of stars
caked in the corners of my eyes.

BLUES FOR DARTH VADER

You stomped the yard of the stars.
When your ship spun out of control, I imagined
the face behind your black mask,
if the expression in your eyes was agonized
or surprised, like my father's were
when my mother told everyone
she was pregnant
again. Like you,
my father had no words:
only evenings and expressways
where overtime shifts and long
commutes home were rewarded
by reheated dinners;
by taking me out
on Halloween night, the two of us
dressed in costumes: me with salt and pepper
shaker lids as eyes for my Tusken Raider mask,
you in your polyester bus-driver work clothes,
walking with me on cracked neighborhood sidewalks
covered in orange candy wrappers and asphalt;
smog massaging your sore back.

BRAND NEW CADILLAC

— after the Clash

Afternoon sun shaving the back
of my sore neck.
The LIE slippery beneath
the round, radial feet

of my father's brand new
Coup de Ville, circa 2002.
The glued face of Jesus beams
with sterling silver gleam

on the dash as we pass sound
walls freshly signed
in muddy ink, like my father's
name on his divorce papers.

The radio speaks, and I'm taken aback:
Joe Strummer is dead.
He ain't never coming back.
Streetlights bow their heads

as if in prayer
to the late December air.

Blue Train

— after John Coltrane

The moon will no longer greet
us at night. Now that another pair of hands rub your back
two rows ahead of me and my knapsack,
your high-pitched cackle makes my ears bleed.

But the damp air of this stop sprays
my hair. I scratch my head and rub my eyes
as the doors open, which reek of burnt Garlic fries,
like the end of days.

The Firmament

When the desert accepted my history,
acknowledged that I had lost

my way, among skyscrapers and sound walls,
like my family — my ancestors in the musty smell of trunks

in boats that crossed the Atlantic from Italia — I searched
for a new home and found a city of crosses: a yucca mecca.

Beth pointed at the Organ Mountains in the distance:
"In the beginning God created Heaven, mesas, and water."

"Who was your first love," Beth asked me.
"When was it?"

"Third Grade, Sophia Marino," I said.
"I dreamt of her pigtails for months."

I stayed in third grade, seated behind Sophia, flicking her pigtails
as if I was learning how to snap my fingers.

My thoughts swam in the cool waters of the desert night,
in the firmament of clouds.

Flea's in-your-face bass wafted through the doorway.
Beth's backyard became our observatory.

The moon was a resort for our hopes.
I never played the pigtails again.

FALSETTO SKY

Here where juniper blossoms
into gin leaves,
I hear the voices of autumn define you
in the silence between the winds
for the first time.
Above short-horned lizards and pecan trees,
the long legs of starlight rub against me.

Yesterday, the thunderheads were an ominous black —
a faint rainbow was distanced behind the mountain peak,
and the clouds let their hair down.

Mountains aren't dazzled; their rocks rasp the moonlight
into fingerfuls of orange peel,
grow into communities
built on land that once flourished
wooden crosses —

My joy
is the thought of us
with the swaying of pine trees.
That sway is their vernacular. That sway,
your vernacular.

I stand here, astonished at how desire chafes;
the splendor wormed by hurt and cruelty,
with scorpions stalking the moon,
and city lights opening their white blouses.

BALLOONS OVER THE SANDIAS

I see hot-air balloons rising above the cactus-clad foothills.
They take a graceful course, their faces tinged in the sun—burning

over a sea of asphalt and flat rooftops;
the coral mesas spreading out under their shadows.

I see the back yard of an adobe house,
in it a dog chews on the cushion of a sofa,

the chamisas on both sides of a road, each cluster,
each flower igniting the day, the cottonwoods brimful with grackles.

Some balloons emerge over the windy piñon summit,
others are just ascending over the tramway—

electric crimson, aquamarine, and circus-peanut orange,
their wicker baskets swaying in the limitless air.

Fly Song

The clouds hold hands. Two flies buzz
on the windowsill of my office.
My head pounding
the backbeat of the morning,
I watch them circle above a vase:
daisies protect me
like yellow, white, and pink umbrellas
from the hard rain of their words.
Then the flies move closer together, like the adobes
down the street, paying no mind to the gritty dusk;
to my love's vermilion bathrobe, bundled on the desk
beside her car and safety deposit box keys;
a ring of reminders that she will return.
The frenetic duet continues.

TREY ANASTASIO AT RED ROCKS AMPHITHEATRE

His guitar clears its throat
onstage. My kid brother
turns 30 tonight.

The stars are frets
pressed by the icy fingertips
of the Rockies. Trey sings

a spirited rendition
of "No Reply at All:"
my thoughts skip

like our sister's Genesis records;
like rocks and stones
across evaporated seas.

What John Romita, Sr. Taught Me

Learning to draw is learning to see.
Start by using bits of plaster
from torn-down buildings

as chalk, then sketch
the Statue of Liberty
on your city street.

One's take on Spider-Man
is another's on Pomodoro Sauce:
ample, robust, developed

after countless attempts and hours
of practice, long after
Christoforo Colombo's name

was Anglicized; long after
Christopher Columbus brought
the tomato back

from the New World; long after
my family migrated from Italia to America.
Let your children sit on your lap

while you work:
humans, cats, and dogs alike.
Comic books can be good for you,

like a glass of red wine every day;
like the Prosciutto, Fig, and Arugula salad
as the first course of Sunday Dinner

at my parents' house.
Look sharp. Don't be afraid
of muscular men, shapely blondes,

red heads, or green goblins. Be yourself,
whether you draw protagonists
with strong chins, or stars

in tonight's sky, soaking
through storm clouds:
an archenemy's glasses.

DEATH STAR SUMMER

Steam rises from the pool. I stand
on the deck, the one
my Cousin Bobby and father built

together. An ambulance siren wails.
I slip, then fall
into the deep end. I see floral patterns, blurry

on the bottom; a ladder rung
out of my reach, like stars above the drive-in
theatre where I saw the back

of Darth Vader's head, without his mask
the previous night. My father grasps
my bony wrist.

Then he wraps me
in a magenta beach towel. I taste
the splashed water of his concerns,

sour with chlorine, and apologize
for scaring him; for diverting
my mother's attention

from his thin lips, curved
in a sneer. When I finish
asking him for forgiveness, I hear

the hoot of an owl, perched somewhere
in the tree above the bug lamp;
the Death Star of his back yard,

electrocuting flies and mosquitoes at will;
their abilities to sing, sting, and love
reduced to a zap here, a crackle there.

I fall asleep. A few hours later,
my father wakes me up
by rubbing my hair

and smiling. He carries me
into the back seat
of his green-gold Pinto

station wagon, our skin bathed
in the car's musty cologne.
We pull out. He rolls down

a window. A breeze wheezes
around us. My father's cigarette
ashes in my eyes.

AVENUE OF THE AMERICAS

I nearly threw up on Joe DiMaggio.

I was 12 years old. My breakfast of pancakes, two fried eggs, home fries, and grapefruit juice churned in my stomach as I inched closer to the front of the line to meet him at a baseball card show in Manhattan. My father, my best friend Matt "Matty-Ass" Fleming and his kid sister Megan accompanied me.

"Don't hunch," my father said. "Remember what we talked about."

Our talk. Two days before, my father had given me specific instructions on how to behave when I met Joe. I was to show no emotion, because he was used to people "swooning like drunken kites" in his presence, and I was "no damned kite." Above all else, I was to address him as "Mr. DiMaggio Sir." Anything less would result in being slapped upside the head so hard I would need to "enlist C. Everett Koop's assistance."

The baseball card show took place at a convention center on Sixth Avenue, officially known as Avenue of the Americas. It was a weekend-long show and featured the autograph sessions of Stan "the Man" Musial and Mr. DiMaggio Sir. Admission for the weekend was $25.00 per day, and for ten dollars more, all attendees had the chance to meet Stan the Man on Saturday and Mr. DiMaggio Sir on Sunday. Stan the

Man would sign just about any baseball-related item, include-ing color photographs, which were $25.00. Mr. DiMaggio Sir wouldn't sign anything involving Marilyn Monroe or Mr. Coffee, a brand of automatic-drip coffee machines.

My father scoffed at the rule. "Fuck that. I drink tea any-way — it's more refined."

Coupled with some commercials Mr. DiMaggio Sir did for Mr. Coffee as its spokesman, my knowledge of him came from watching Yankees Old-Timers' Day games on TV as a child with my father and Grandfather Joe. Although I recall little about the games themselves, two details stick with me: first, of all the retired players gathered at Yankee Stadium, Mr. DiMaggio Sir was always the last player introduced in the pre-game ceremonies. Second, I didn't understand why such was the case.

I learned in time. For my father, Mr. DiMaggio Sir's base-ball career was characterized by his Major League record 56-game hitting streak, his Pacific Coast League record 61-game hitting streak as a member of the San Francisco Seals, and being referenced by Simon and Garfunkel in the song Mrs. Robinson. "Even hippies respect the guy," my father said.

I also discovered that the most important aspect of Mr. DiMaggio Sir's high standing with my family was because he was the son of Italian immigrants, a *paesano* who went from cleaning dead fish off his father's boat in San Francisco to patrolling center field in Yankee Stadium. In addition to having won 3 Most Valuable Player awards, 13 All Star selections, and 9 World Series championship rings during his storied baseball career, Joe was also venerated in the Nicoletti household because he lost three years of his career to World War Two, having enlisted in the U.S. Army Air Forces. This made him a brother-in-arms to both of my grandfathers, who also fought in the war: my grandfather Joe for the USA, and my Nonno Giovanni for Italia. Like them, Mr. DiMaggio Sir served his country proudly, despite the fact that his parents were classified as enemy aliens along with thousands of other Americans of Italian and Japanese descent by the US government after Pearl Harbor was attacked by Japan. He achieved the rank of Sergeant and was inducted into the National Baseball Hall of Fame in 1955.

While other Italian-American athletes had also achieved worldwide fame and fortune in the 1950's, such as the Heavyweight Champion boxer Rocky Marciano, Mr. DiMaggio Sir was arguably the first to transcend his sport, which for my family was best exemplified by his marriage to Marilyn Monroe. That Marilyn filed for divorce on the grounds of "mental cruelty" 274 days after their wedding didn't matter. By winning the hand and heart of an actress who was as famous for being a sex symbol as she was for her comedic and dramatic talents, Mr. DiMaggio Sir had demonstrated that there was more to him than the ability to hit a baseball with consistency and to pick it in the field like a boss. The way my father and grandfather saw it, he had a sense of honor. Being the son of blue-collar workers was something to be proud of: in Mr. DiMaggio Sir's case a fisherman, in my father's case, a bus driver for the Metropolitan Transit Authority. Like wearing the uniform of the US Army, or Yankee pinstripes, America was a good fit for people of Italian descent.

Further, Mr. DiMaggio Sir had "class." As devastated as he reportedly was by Marilyn's death in 1962, he handled all the funeral arrangements. He famously forbade all of Hollywood's elite to attend, choosing to limit attendance to close friends and relatives, and had six red roses sent to her crypt three times a week for two decades. To my parents' and grandparents' way of thinking, Mr. DiMaggio Sir's on and off the field successes legitimized the relevance of Italians in American popular culture as positive influences on young people, particularly men. As Grandfather Joe put it, "Better to have my sons make their mark as a centerfielder for Joe McCarthy than as a hitman for Al Capone."

So there I was on Sunday, trying not to have a Technicolor yawn. The combination of breakfast, the rigidity of my father's instructions, and my own excitement had wreaked havoc on my stomach and sanity. I took deep breaths to calm myself down. Alas.

Instead, I focused on Paul Carrack's blue-eyed, soulful lead vocal on the song "Tempted," which was booming from a monolithic-sized stereo speaker mounted above the doorway.

I made my way to the center of the table, where Mr. DiMaggio Sir was sitting. A resplendent figure, he looked even more regal in person than he did on TV. Neither the scuffed Maplewood wall panels or the braids of cigarette smoke squirming like faceless snakes around the ceiling fan could remove the shine of his white hair, parted to the left, or the red stripes of his silk tie. His shirt was starched, impeccable, which was complimented by a navy-blue blazer. He smiled as he looked down at me, lips glistening with the elegance of a bona-fide baseball deity, whom my father could not have wanted me to believe in more.

"Hello young man," he said. "What's your name?"

My stomach gurgled, as if in response. I coughed, trying to cover it up.

"Stalin. Joseph Stallin,'" Matty-Ass quipped.

Paul Carrack kept giving me his vocal medicine.

"Good after-n-noon, Mr. Duh-Duh-Maggio Sir. My name is Joey. H-how you doin' today?"

Mr. DiMaggio Sir allowed himself a little laugh. "Why, I'm doing just fine, Joey. Thanks for asking. Would you like me to sign your baseball?"

Goose pimples bloomed on my arms. I didn't have a baseball with me. In fact, I didn't have any items that would be appropriate for an occasion like this. I tried to think on my feet.

"W-well, I don't have a ball—a baseball, that is, b-but I have this."

I removed and unfolded a creased copy of the show flyer from my pants pocket. My hands trembled as I placed the flyer on the table. It felt like distance between San Francisco and Manhattan.

Mr. DiMaggio Sir furrowed his brow.

"Forgive me for asking, Joey, but where's your picture? Didn't the man give you one?"

"W-Which man?"

My father slapped the back of my head. "Mojo!"

I listened for the music, but there was none. Mr. DiMaggio Sir stared at the flyer.

"Of course you don't have a picture of me. You've been having fun at the show, buying cards and what not. Am I right?"

Then I saw Mr. DiMaggio Sir motion to a bald man in a black suit and steel-gray fedora standing at the right end of the table. He looked like a shorter version of the actor Telly Savalas as Detective Theo Kojak, minus the lollipop or flair for catchphrases.

"Could you please give my friend *Joey* a picture?"

Kojak's nostrils flared. "Nope."

Mr. DiMaggio Sir's right eyebrow rose. "I beg your pardon?"

"He didn't pay his fee."

"Come again?"

"No 25 bucks, no picture. House rules."

Mr. DiMaggio Sir shook his head, and then held my hand. I felt my lungs photosynthesize.

"How old are you, Joey?"

"I'm t-twelve."

Mr. DiMaggio Sir turned his head to Kojak. "What twelve-year old has 25 dollars to spend on a photograph of an athlete who they never saw play?"

"Like I said, house—"

"It's bad enough that you're making as much money as you are off these fans, especially the youngsters. Please, give Joey a picture. Now," Mr. DiMaggio Sir said. He nodded at me.

Kojak scowled the eyes out of my sockets. Who hates ya, baby?

"Here you go, Kid. I'm sorry, Mr. DiMaggio."

"You should be, "Kojak-off," Matty-Ass hollered.

I heard a medley of applause and whistles. Kojak took a large swig of his Yoo-Hoo, almost draining the bottle.

"How should I sign this for you, Joey?"

I said the only thought that came to mind. "With a blue-inked pen, please?"

Mr. DiMaggio, Sir flashed the radiant smile that sold thousands of coffee machines and won Marilyn Monroe's gorgeous hand in marriage.

"How about, 'To Joey, best wishes, Joe DiMaggio?'"

"Sure. That works."

Mr. DiMaggio laughed as he signed my picture. I smiled when the rest of the band members of Squeeze picked up from where Paul had left off.

Then my father took the lead.

"Uh, Joe? Mr. D? How are ya? Would it be okay if you and Mojo posed for a picture or two? I'm his *padre*, so it's not child abductor behavior at work here. Would that be okay?"

"Sure, Mr..."

"Nicoletti. Joe Nicoletti."

"It would be my pleasure, Mr. Nicoletti. Take as many as you would like."

"Call me Joe."

Before I knew it, Kojak had escorted me behind the table, where I stood behind Mr. DiMaggio Sir, looking on as he signed Matty-Ass's, Megan's, and other people's items. Memories of it still keep calling.

After countless poses and camera flashes, Matty–Ass and I handed our autographed pictures to my father. He put them in a manila envelope. Finally, on to the baseball card hunt.

"I hereby release the hounds. See you in two hours," he said, pointing at the door behind him.

"By the Men's Room?" Megan asked.

"At the water fountain. In two hours."

***

Megan, Matty-Ass and I searched and discovered; we bargained to our heart's desires, all of my 15 dollars of it; to Megan's and Matty-Ass's combined 63 dollars. By the end of the day, Megan and Matty-Ass had scored a 1957 Jackie Robinson card in pristine condition.

I was equally excited, having purchased the rookie card of Ken Singleton, my favorite living ballplayer, for a dollar. I came across some cards of Mr. DiMaggio Sir, but none of them fit my budget.

Matty-Ass and I met front of the rest room. There was no sign of my father. Megan was already there, drinking from the fountain.

An elevator door slid open behind where Matty-Ass was standing. Mr. DiMaggio Sir and two other men emerged, their blood-shot eyes glued on my father, who was in rare form.

"So the priest says, 'Hey, wait a minute. That's not a rooster!'"

Everyone in the group burst out laughing. So did Megan. Matty-Ass and I were flabbergasted.

"Good one, Joe," Mr. DiMaggio Sir said. His tie was loose.

"You know it — Joe!"

More laughter. My father's thunderous chuckle could have been heard back home on Teed Street. Mr. DiMaggio Sir slapped my father's back.

"Mister Nick," Megan called.

"Oh yeah. It was great talkin' with ya, Joe. Say hi to Yogi for me."

"Yogi?" Matty-Ass asked Megan and me. "As in Berra?"

"No, as in Mussolini," Megan replied.

My father and Mr. DiMaggio Sir shook hands. "Take care. It was a pleasure meeting all of you."

Mr. DiMaggio Sir and I shared a smile. Then he and the other two men walked back into the elevator. My father swaggered towards Matty-Ass, Megan and me, the ding of the elevator bell resounding through the hallway as the doors closed.

WHAT RINGO STARR TAUGHT ME

It's okay to leave
the company of the Maharishi
if the food is too spicy.

So you're no star,
anyone can make a difference
if the rhythm's right.

Yes, we're all drummers,
beating the big bass
of pleasure and pain.

And when your group breaks up
like my parents, go solo,
just like Ringo.

It's Tricky

— after Run DMC

My head hurts. Instead of Aspirin, I find relief
in the plan I'm concocting:
I'll take the subway to work from now on.
A portion of my paychecks will be put aside
for my son's new pair of glasses, so he can see
his favorite planetarium ceiling
on his next birthday. I'll chew gum
when I crave a cigarette;
breathe a tiny sigh of regret
when I leave my vicinity
of graffiti and power lines behind.
The beats of Run DMC will leak
from my ears. One good grain of rain will take.
The turnstiles and I will embrace.

THE DEATH OF BOBA FETT

July 4th. Cousin Lenny hurls
my kid brother's Boba Fett
action figure into the burning barbeque grill.
I clench my hand into a fist,

then taste the bitter flavor
of my own blood. Nothing can mend
his favorite toy; the yellow fever
of sparklers. Fireworks speak their mind:

the sky is alight with a gold choir
of booming voices. When I look on
from my avocado-green lawn chair,
sparks go off between fireworks and the moon.

EARTHQUAKE WEATHER

In the place where we were half-right,
Pickups wore jackets of mist.
The oily smell of the refinery festered
like a boil on the neck of town.

In the place where we were half-right,
houses were made of sleet;
vine climbed the spines of chimneys.

We planted our hopes and dreams
in the back yard, like squirrels who hide
nuts and seeds, only to forget
where they buried them.

Sleep rained down every Christmas
Eve. Perhaps a murmur can be heard
where our tool shed used to stand.

1980 FUTURE STARS

Buffalo. My new home. I unpack a box.
The dog comes running
with a creased baseball card
in his mouth: 1980 Future Stars,
New York Mets. I remove it
from his jowls and read
the back. Dan Norman.
Outfielder. We share a birthday:
January 11th. We share a borough:
Queens. His life in the show began
in Flushing, in Big Shea. My life began
in Astoria General Hospital.
Both structures have been replaced.
Dan throws and bats right, just as I used to
when I played games of pickup stickball;
my childhood streets awash in the oily aroma
of fried eggplant, wafting
from open windows. Teenaged boys talk smack.
Comebacks. Mine undermined
by garlicky breath. Popped zits. But today, I regard
my new neighborhood. Gusts of wind rattle
rusted dumpsters in my building's parking lot.
People scream as a roller coaster train drops
in the distance. My phone rings.
I put the card in my pocket. Behind shoreline clouds,
the sun, a sand dollar, depreciates.

Old World Soufflé

If I was a French chef
and you were hungry for croissants
I would take my finest dough and roll them
into existence for you.
Martha Stewart would nod at me
with approval.
Giada DeLaurentis and Jacques Pepin would taste them
and be as pleased as lovers
necking in a drive-in theatre.

Do people still neck?
Aren't drive-ins all but extinct?
It's perfectly fine to ask,
though Giada is married and Jacques lives part of the year in F

where, if we had lived over 200 years ago,
I would have been a peasant storming the Bastille
and have sent my dog
to pick up your scent in the towers of the fortress
before it blazed
like an old world soufflé.

Later, after drinking several bottles of wine,
I would have taken you to Venice
rowed a gondola down its wet streets

and put my hand up your shirt
amidst the villas and cathedrals
built on piles sunk deep into mud.

Under the Milky Way

– after the Church

The sky is a stein glass, streaked
with ice. I'm listening
to Peter Koppes's guitar,
strumming from the jukebox,
and people fill the patio like cars in a lot
for a tailgate party. Despite my best efforts,
my thoughts are bumper to bumper
in the gridlock of my concerns;
of not knowing
where my next paycheck will come from;
when my former students will be allowed to come home
from the sands of Afghanistan;
why my father has been coughing up blood
for the past week. The patron's cheers
pops in corn, salty behind the bar
as Marshawn Lynch goes into Beast Mode, then crosses
the goal line on the big screen:
my semi-private consultation.
I feel like the closed steel mill smokestack
my wife and I passed on our way here:
my sooty throat sore;
veiled in the shadow of a rusted skyline
until Steve Kilbey sings

Something that's shimmering and white
Leads you here despite your destination
Under the Milky Way tonight.
I am at this bar and grill, under the weather
of my personal Milky Way tonight;
in search of another workplace
hospitable to life
as I would like to know it;
where there sound of my breath
fades with streetlight less often,
where trees refuse to give up their leaves
for the chump change
of October wind and drizzle.
Until such time, I take refuge
in various forms of comfort and amusement:
a night out with friends and family;
a Seattle Seahawks victory;
a drink served to my wife
by a doe-eyed waitress;
or in my case, a Diet Coke,
an Advil and a favorite tune:
some over and beyond-the-counter medicine
to cure at least part
of what ails me today.
It's only a matter of time
until it takes effect;
until someone scribbles
their phone number on someone else's palm;
a tattoo of sweaty possibility;
until somebody scores

another touchdown, a smash hit;
until the fuzzy head of a new song
emerges from the jukebox's neon womb.

WINTER LAGER

Mercury peeks out of a cloud
like a diamond stud
on an earlobe of sky.
My best friend died
a year ago tonight.
An empty beer bottle rolls
on the ground behind his pine:
Samuel Adams Winter Lager.
My youngest and I step
onto a cracked sidewalk,
blanketed by bile-yellow
fast-food wrappers and moonlight.
The bottle keeps moving.
I wish I could say that
the same has been true for me
these past 12 months.
Car alarms and horns
ring and honk in a parking lot
across the street. No one responds
save my youngest,
whose bombastic bark falls in rainwater
from a rusted gutter
before it fades
in a patch of crab grass.

THE SPOT

Snowflakes spit out of clouds
like slot machine coins. The dog
scratches my leg;
he wants to go
to his favorite patch of grass
and roll on his back, mindless of the sleet;
the insipid hissing of geese
next door. The wind
howls the vowels
of my old flame's name.
We reach the spot. He tastes
a stick, crunchy with frost,
then squats behind his leafless oak.
I have only been here
for a few months, but my soul feels
as bare as his tree. My new home is
a building, aromatic
with the salty smoke of country ham,
where doors slam and neighbors watch
over each other's pets: the latest
tenants who have put down roots
in my nomadic heart.

Reverse Graffiti

The moon is a communion wafer, cracked
above the Manhattan skyline. A lanky
woman brushes dust, grime, and soot
off the side of a building. A new one
emerges: One World
Trade Center. The alley
dimly lit, perfumed with detergent,
like my mother's hands, on the day
she collapsed, and went
to Mount Sinai Hospital, never
to return. I cry. The evening speaks
in raspy neon air, urging,
rise, rise, rise.

JOEY NICOLETTI was born in Astoria, Queens, and holds a BA from the University of Iowa, an MA from New Mexico State University, and earned his MFA in Poetry Writing from Sarah Lawrence College.

A poet, memoirist, playwright, and essayist, his work has been nominated for a Pushcart Prize and has appeared in various literary journals and anthologies, including *Voices in Italian Americana, Jet Fuel Review, Gradiva, Valparaiso Poetry Review, Aethlon: the Journal of Sport Literature,* and *Drawn to Marvel: Poems from the Comic Books.* The author of four poetry collections, *Cannoli Gangster,* his first book, was selected as a finalist for the Steel Toe Books Poetry Prize.

He is a former Poetry Editor of *Puerto del Sol* and serves on the Executive Committee of the Italian American Studies Association. Joey currently resides in Western New York with his family, where he teaches and tutors writing at SUNY Buffalo State, and roots for the Seattle Seahawks. He can be found online at www.joeynicoletti.com.

VIA FOLIOS

A refereed book series dedicated to the culture of Italians and Italian Americans.

Bordighera Press is an imprint of Bordighera, Incorporated, an independently owned not-for-profit scholarly organization that has no legal affiliation with the University of Central Florida or with The John D. Calandra Italian American Institute, Queens College/CUNY.

HELEN BAROLINI, *Crossing the Alps*, Vol. 65, Fiction, $14

COSMO FERRARA, *Profiles of Italian Americans*, Vol. 64, Italian Americana, $16

GIL FAGIANI, *Chianti in Connecticut*, Vol. 63, Poetry, $10

BASSETTI & D'ACQUINO, *Italic Lessons*, Vol. 62, Italian/American Studies, $10

CAVALIERI & PASCARELLI, Eds., *The Poet's Cookbook*, Vol. 61, Poetry/Recipes, $12

EMANUEL DI PASQUALE, *Siciliana*, Vol. 60, Poetry, $8

NATALIA COSTA, Ed., *Bufalini*, Vol. 59, Poetry. $18.

RICHARD VETERE, *Baroque*, Vol. 58, Fiction. $18.

LEWIS TURCO, *La Famiglia/The Family*, Vol. 57, Memoir, $15

NICK JAMES MILETI, *The Unscrupulous*, Vol. 56, Humanities, $20

BASSETTI, ACCOLLA, D'AQUINO, *Italici: An Encounter with Piero Bassetti*, Vol. 55, Italian Studies, $8

GIOSE RIMANELLI, *The Three-legged One*, Vol. 54, Fiction, $15

CHARLES KLOPP, *Bele Antiche Stòrie*, Vol. 53, Criticism, $25

JOSEPH RICAPITO, *Second Wave*, Vol. 52, Poetry, $12

GARY MORMINO, *Italians in Florida*, Vol. 51, History, $15

GIANFRANCO ANGELUCCI, *Federico F.*, Vol. 50, Fiction, $15

ANTHONY VALERIO, *The Little Sailor*, Vol. 49, Memoir, $9

ROSS TALARICO, *The Reptilian Interludes*, Vol. 48, Poetry, $15

RACHEL GUIDO DE VRIES, *Teeny Tiny Tino's Fishing Story*, Vol. 47, Children's Literature, $6

EMANUEL DI PASQUALE, *Writing Anew*, Vol. 46, Poetry, $15

MARIA FAMÀ, *Looking For Cover*, Vol. 45, Poetry, $12

ANTHONY VALERIO, *Toni Cade Bambara's One Sicilian Night*, Vol. 44, Poetry, $10

EMANUEL CARNEVALI, Dennis Barone, Ed., *Furnished Rooms*, Vol. 43, Poetry, $14

BRENT ADKINS, et al., Ed., *Shifting Borders, Negotiating Places*, Vol. 42, Proceedings, $18

GEORGE GUIDA, *Low Italian*, Vol. 41, Poetry, $11

GARDAPHÈ, GIORDANO, TAMBURRI, *Introducing Italian Americana*, Vol. 40, Italian/American Studies, $10

DANIELA GIOSEFFI, *Blood Autumn/Autunno di sangue*, Vol. 39, Poetry, $15/$25

FRED MISURELLA, *Lies to Live by*, Vol. 38, Stories, $15

STEVEN BELLUSCIO, *Constructing a Bibliography*, Vol. 37, Italian Americana, $15

ANTHONY JULIAN TAMBURRI, Ed., *Italian Cultural Studies 2002*, Vol. 36, Essays, $18

BEA TUSIANI, *con amore*, Vol. 35, Memoir, $19

FLAVIA BRIZIO-SKOV, Ed., *Reconstructing Societies in the Aftermath of War*, Vol. 34, History, $30

TAMBURRI, et al., Eds., *Italian Cultural Studies 2001*, Vol. 33, Essays, $18

ELIZABETH G. MESSINA, Ed., *In Our Own Voices*, Vol. 32, Italian/American Studies, $25

STANISLAO G. PUGLIESE, *Desperate Inscriptions*, Vol. 31, History, $12

HOSTERT & TAMBURRI, Eds., *Screening Ethnicity*, Vol. 30, Italian/American Culture, $25

G. PARATI & B. LAWTON, Eds., *Italian Cultural Studies*, Vol. 29, Essays, $18

HELEN BAROLINI, *More Italian Hours*, Vol. 28, Fiction, $16

FRANCO NASI, Ed., *Intorno alla Via Emilia*, Vol. 27, Culture, $16

ARTHUR L. CLEMENTS, *The Book of Madness & Love*, Vol. 26, Poetry, $10

JOHN CASEY, et al., *Imagining Humanity*, Vol. 25, Interdisciplinary Studies, $18

ROBERT LIMA, *Sardinia/Sardegna*, Vol. 24, Poetry, $10

DANIELA GIOSEFFI, *Going On*, Vol. 23, Poetry, $10

ROSS TALARICO, *The Journey Home*, Vol. 22, Poetry, $12

EMANUEL DI PASQUALE, *The Silver Lake Love Poems*, Vol. 21, Poetry, $7

JOSEPH TUSIANI, *Ethnicity*, Vol. 20, Poetry, $12

JENNIFER LAGIER, *Second Class Citizen*, Vol. 19, Poetry, $8

FELIX STEFANILE, *The Country of Absence*, Vol. 18, Poetry, $9